STORIES FROM CENTRAL AMERICA / CUENTOS DE CENTROAMÉRICA

MOTHER SCORPION COUNTRY
LA TIERRA DE LA MADRE ESCORPIÓN

A Legend from the Miskito Indians of Nicaragua / *Una Leyenda de los Indios Miskitos de Nicaragua*

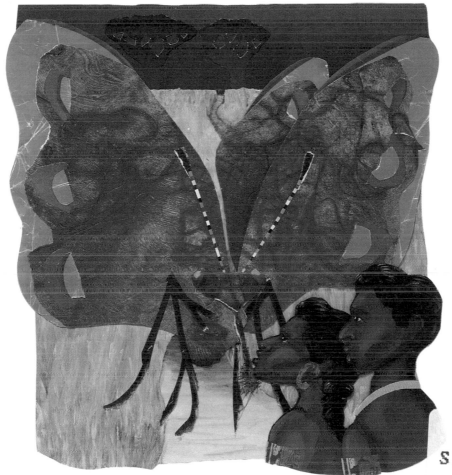

Harriet Rohmer · Dorminster Wilson

Illustrations / Ilustraciones — Virginia Stearns

Version in Spanish / Versión en español — Rosalma Zubizarreta & Alma Flor Ada

Dedicated to June Beer: painter, poet and storyteller from
  Bluefields, Nicaragua. We miss you.
Dedicado a June Beer: pintora, poeta y cuentista de Bluefields, Nicaragua.
  Te extrañamos.

Art/Production Consultant: Robin Cherin
Design: Naomi Schiff, Seventeenth Street Studios
Photography: Joe Samberg

Printed in the U.S.A.

Library of Congress Cataloging-in-Publication Data

Rohmer, Harriet.
  Mother Scorpion country.
  (Stories from Central America = Cuentos de
Centroamérica)
  English and Spanish.
  Summary: A brave young Miskito Indian follows his
wife from the land of the living to the spirit world.
  1. Mosquito Indians—Legends. 2. Indians of Central
America—Nicaragua—Legends. [1. Mosquito Indians—Legends.
2. Indians of Central America—Nicaragua—Legends. 3. Spanish language
materials—Bilingual] I. Wilson, Dorminster Newton. II. Stearns,
Virginia, ill. III. Title. IV. Title: Tierra de la
Madre Escorpión. V. Series: Stories from Central
America.
F1529.M9R65 1987   398.2'08997   86-32649
ISBN 0-89239-032-8

Long ago in the land of the Miskitos, there lived a woman called Kati and her husband Naklili who loved her very much.

Hace mucho tiempo, en la tierra de los miskitos, vivían una mujer llamada Kati y su esposo Naklili. Naklili quería muchísimo a Kati.

One day Kati got very sick. Soon afterward she died, but Naklili refused to be separated from her.

He built a coffin large enough for both of them and he dug the grave himself. Then he went to his house and got some fresh chicken eggs and cassava for the two of them to eat. He took his reed flute and his lance. Then he was ready.

At the funeral Naklili watched over Kati as she was placed in the coffin and carried to the grave. When the coffin was set down, Naklili got into it beside Kati. Then he commanded his relatives to nail down the cover and bury them together.

They begged him to change his mind, but Naklili refused. At last, they did as he said. They buried him with his dead wife.

Un día, Kati se puso muy enferma. Poco después, murió. Pero Naklili no quería separarse de ella.

Naklili construyó un ataúd suficientemente grande para que cupieran los dos y cavó la fosa él mismo. Luego fue a su casa y buscó huevos de gallina y un poco de yuca para comer los dos. Tomó su flauta de bambú y su lanza. Así se preparó.

Durante el entierro, Naklili observaba cómo ponían a Kati en el ataúd y la llevaban a la tumba. Cuando bajaron el ataúd, Naklili se metió dentro, al lado de Kati. Luego ordenó a sus familiares que cerraran el ataúd y los enterraran juntos.

Los familiares le rogaron que no tomase esa decisión, pero Naklili se mantuvo firme. Por fin, hicieron lo que él pedía. Lo enterraron con su esposa muerta.

In the grave Naklili continued watching over Kati. When a mouse came to nibble at her foot, he killed it with his lance. When an opossum came and ants came, he killed them too.

After awhile Naklili noticed that Kati's big toe moved. Then her feet moved. Soon her whole body started shaking and she began to sit up. Then she saw Naklili.

"Why are you here?" she cried.

"I love you and I want to go wherever you go," answered Naklili.

"You cannot go with me," said Kati. "I belong to the dead. You must remain with the living."

En la tumba, Naklili continuó vigilando a Kati. Cuando un ratón vino a mordisquearle un pie, él lo mató con su lanza. Cuando vinieron primero una zarigüeya y, luego, unas hormigas, las mató también.

Después de un tiempo, Naklili se dio cuenta de que el dedo gordo del pie de Kati se movía. Luego se movieron los pies. Muy pronto todo el cuerpo de Kati estaba temblando y ella se comenzó a sentar. Entonces vio a Naklili.

—¿Qué haces aquí? —gritó.

—Yo te quiero y deseo ir adondequiera que tú vayas —le contestó Naklili.

—No puedes venir conmigo —le dijo Kati—. Yo pertenezco a los muertos. Tú tienes que permanecer con los vivos.

No, I will not leave you," said Naklili.

Kati was silent for a long time. "If you come with me it will be very difficult for you," she said at last.

"I am not afraid," replied Naklili.

Again Kati was silent for a long time. Finally she said, "Close your eyes and take my hand. You must not open your eyes until I tell you to."

Naklili obeyed. He felt himself rise from the coffin and fly through the air beside Kati. They flew for what seemed like a long time and many troubling thoughts came to him. At last, his thoughts came to rest.

No, no te dejaré —contestó Naklili.

Kati se quedó callada por mucho tiempo. —Si vienes conmigo, va a ser muy difícil para ti —dijo al fin.

—No tengo miedo —respondió Naklili.

Otra vez Kati se quedó callada por largo rato. Por fin dijo: —Cierra los ojos y dame la mano. No debes abrir los ojos hasta que te diga que los abras.

Naklili obedeció. Sintió que se elevaba del ataúd y que volaba por el aire al lado de Kati. Volaron por lo que pareció un largo rato y muchos pensamientos difíciles le llenaban la mente. Por fin, sus pensamientos pudieron descansar.

Y ou can open your eyes," said Kati. They were on a road that led westward through a beautiful, grassy plain. Kati told Naklili to follow her.

They walked and walked until they came to a giant butterfly blocking the road. Its enormous wings kept opening and closing, opening and closing, threatening to crush them if they tried to pass. Kati guided them around the danger.

On and on they walked until they came to a bridge as narrow as a hair. The bridge was guarded by a toothless demon, waiting to hurl them into the boiling sea below. Again Kati guided them around the danger.

P uedes abrir los ojos —le dijo Kati. Estaban en un camino que iba hacia el oeste a través de una hermosa pradera. Kati le dijo a Naklili que la siguiera.

Caminaron y caminaron hasta que encontraron una mariposa gigantesca que interrumpía todo el camino. Sus alas enormes se abrían y cerraban, se abrían y cerraban, amenazando aplastarlos si trataban de pasar. Kati los guió para evitar el peligro.

Siguieron caminando y caminando hasta que llegaron a un puente tan estrecho como un pelo. Un demonio sin dientes vigilaba el puente y esperaba arrojarlos al mar hirviente que había debajo. Otra vez, Kati los guió para que evitaran el peligro.

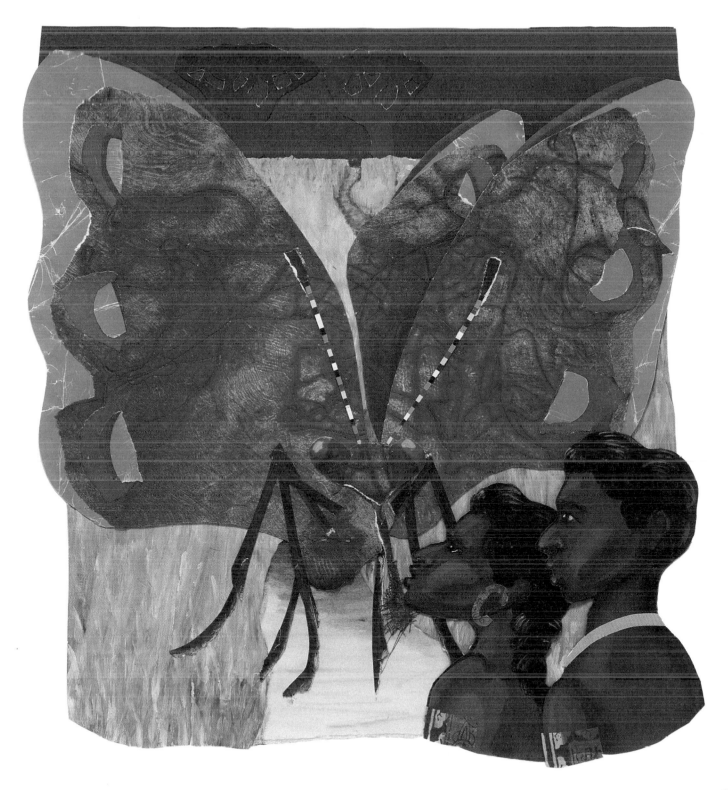

The road turned northward, bringing them to the shores of a large lagoon. On the other side of the lagoon lay Mother Scorpion Country, the land of the dead.

Naklili lighted a fire and began to prepare the eggs and cassava he had brought. But Kati did not want his food.

"I will find some tasty tortoises," she said. And she disappeared into the marsh. But she did not return with tortoises.

"Those are black bugs! They're tortoise-shaped black bugs!" cried Naklili in disgust.

"No, they are tortoises!" insisted Kati. She roasted and ate them. Naklili had to eat his food alone.

El camino volteó hacia el norte, trayéndolos al borde de un lago grande. Al otro lado del lago se encontraba la Tierra de la Madre Escorpión, la tierra de los muertos.

Naklili encendió fuego y comenzó a cocinar los huevos y la yuca que había traído. Pero Kati no quiso compartir su comida.

—Encontraré unas ricas tortugas —dijo. Y desapareció en el pantano. Pero cuando regresó no traía tortugas.

—¡Esos son escarabajos negros! ¡Son insectos en forma de tortuga! —gritó Naklili disgustado.

—¡No! Son tortugas —insistió Kati. Y asó los animales y se los comió. Naklili tuvo que comerse su comida solo.

After they had eaten, Kati called to the other side of the lagoon for someone to come and take her across. Moments later they saw a small boat moving quickly toward them. Naklili hid in the bushes with his lance ready.

A short distance away the boat stopped.

"Why don't you land the boat?" called Kati.

"Because the smell of the living is there!" replied the boatman.

"No, I am alone here!" said Kati.

The boat drifted toward her. Suddenly, Naklili sprang from behind the bush. The terrified boatman jumped into the water and started swimming away. In amazement Naklili realized that the boatman was really a frog.

Después que hubieron comido, Kati llamó al otro lado del lago para que viniera alguien a ayudarla a cruzar. Unos minutos más tarde, vieron una barca pequeña que venía rápidamente hacia ellos. Naklili se escondió detrás de unas matas, con la lanza lista.

La barca se detuvo a alguna distancia de la orilla.

—¿Por qué no atracan la barca? —preguntó Kati.

—¡Porque hay olor a seres vivientes! —respondió el barquero.

—¡No! No hay nadie más que yo aquí —dijo Kati.

La barca empezó a acercarse a ella. De repente, Naklili saltó de detrás de las matas. El barquero, asustadísimo, saltó al agua y empezó a nadar para alejarse. Sorprendido, Naklili se dio cuenta que el barquero era en realidad una rana.

B

e careful," warned Kati as she got into the boat with Naklili. "There are sharks in this water."

"Those are not sharks," said Naklili, "only sardines."

"No, they are sharks," said Kati.

Naklili paddled on in silence. As they neared the shores of Mother Scorpion Country, they heard singing and shouting. The spirits were already celebrating Kati's arrival.

Mother Scorpion, a large woman far taller than Naklili, waded into the water and pulled their boat onto the beach. She embraced Kati and wept for joy. Other spirits lifted Kati onto their shoulders and carried her away to the feasting and dancing.

Mother Scorpion turned angrily to Naklili. "Who are you?"

T

en cuidado —le advirtió Kati a Naklili, cuando subieron a la barca—. Hay tiburones en este lago.

—Esos no son tiburones —dijo Naklili—. Son sólo sardinas.

—¡No! Son tiburones —dijo Kati.

Naklili remó en silencio. Cuando llegaron a la orilla de la Tierra de la Madre Escorpión, escucharon cantos y gritos. Los espíritus ya estaban celebrando la llegada de Kati.

La Madre Escorpión, una mujer grande, mucho más alta que Naklili, entró al agua para halar la barca hasta la playa. Abrazó a Kati y lloró de alegría. Otros espíritus alzaron a Kati y se la llevaron en hombros para que tomara parte en el festejo y el baile.

La Madre Escorpión se volvió hacia Naklili, muy enojada. —¿Quién eres?

17

I am Kati's husband," replied Naklili.

"You have no right to be here. You belong to the world of the living. You must return there immediately."

"But I cannot leave my wife," said Naklili.

Mother Scorpion's anger faded. She was moved by Naklili's love for Kati.

"You may stay here," she said, "but you will never be able to forget that you are different from us. This land is a paradise for the spirits, but it will be ugly and lonely for you."

Kati tried to be kind to Naklili. When they strolled together through Mother Scorpion Country, she pointed happily to the trees filled with golden bananas and ripe coconuts.

Soy el esposo de Kati —contestó Naklili.

—No tienes ningún derecho a estar aquí. Tú perteneces al mundo de los vivos. Tienes que regresar allí inmediatamente.

—Pero no puedo dejar a mi esposa —dijo Naklili.

La furia de la Madre Escorpión se desvaneció. Estaba conmovida por el amor de Naklili por Kati.

—Te puedes quedar —dijo—, pero nunca podrás olvidar que no eres como nosotros. Esta tierra es un paraíso para los espíritus, pero para ti será fea y solitaria.

Kati trató de ayudar a Naklili. Cuando caminaban juntos por la Tierra de la Madre Escorpión, le señalaba alegremente los árboles cargados de plátanos dorados y cocos maduros.

But Naklili could not see the golden bananas or the ripe coconuts. All he saw were the skeletons of trees that had died centuries before.

"Listen to the yellowtail birds!" Kati would say. And she imitated their song: "Kik-kik! Kik-kik!"

But Naklili could not hear the birds. He heard only a harsh, rattling sound like the breath of a dying man.

Naklili was very sad. At last he understood. He could walk with Kati in her land of delight, but he could never share her happiness.

"Kati," he said. "Is there a way for me to return to the land of the living?"

Pero Naklili no podía ver los plátanos dorados ni los cocos maduros. Todo lo que veía eran los esqueletos de árboles que habían muerto hacía siglos.

—Escucha los pájaros de cola amarilla —decía Kati. E imitaba su canción: —¡Quic-quic! ¡Quic-quic!

Pero Naklili no podía oír a los pájaros. Oía sólo un ruido desagradable y áspero, como la respiración de un moribundo.

Naklili se entristeció mucho. Por fin comprendió. Podía caminar con su querida Kati en su tierra paradisíaca, pero nunca podría compartir su felicidad.

Kati —le dijo—. ¿Hay alguna forma de poder regresar a la tierra de los vivos?

"I can send you back," said Kati.

"But how?" asked Naklili.

Kati looked at him sadly. "Follow me quietly," she said.

On the beach she found the trunk of a large bamboo tree. She cut it open and told Naklili to climb inside.

"Say nothing about what you have seen here until you are ready to return to me," she said. "Then, call all your relatives together and tell your story. When you have finished, take the string of beads that I have left for you above the door."

Kati gazed at Naklili for a few last moments. Then she closed the bamboo, leaving one small hole, and set it adrift.

Y o te puedo mandar de regreso —dijo Kati.

—Pero, ¿cómo? —preguntó Naklili.

Kati lo miró tristemente. —Sígueme en silencio —le dijo.

En la playa, Kati encontró un grueso tronco de bambú. Lo partió y le dijo a Naklili que se metiera dentro.

—No le cuentes nada a nadie de lo que has visto acá hasta que estés listo para regresar a mi lado —le dijo—. Entonces reúne a todos tus familiares y cuéntales tu historia. Cuando acabes, toma el collar de cuentas que he dejado para ti encima de la puerta.

Kati miró a Naklili por unos últimos minutos. Luego cerró el bambú, dejando un pequeño agujero y lo echó a flotar.

The bamboo drifted on and on carried by the tide until it landed on the beach near Naklili's home. In the distance Naklili saw his sister. He began to play his flute.

"That's my brother's flute!" she cried. She ran toward the sound which seemed to come from inside the bamboo. Carefully, she split open the bamboo with her machete.

"Naklili!"

Brother and sister hugged each other joyfully. Arm in arm they started for home. Naklili played his flute so all his relatives could hear. They knew immediately it was Naklili, the man they had buried alive with his dead wife. Naklili's mother greeted him with open arms. Then the relatives arrived and stared in wonder.

El bambú flotó y flotó, llevado por la corriente, hasta que llegó a la playa cercana a la casa de Naklili. A la distancia, Naklili vio a su hermana. Comenzó a tocar la flauta.

—¡Ésa es la flauta de mi hermano! —gritó ella. Corrió hacia el sonido que parecía venir de adentro del bambú. Cuidadosamente, abrió el bambú con su machete.

—¡Naklili!

Hermano y hermana se abrazaron de alegría. Y cogidos del brazo regresaron a la casa. Naklili tocaba la flauta para que todos sus familiares le escucharan. Supieron inmediatamente que era Naklili, el hombre que habían enterrado junto a su esposa muerta. La madre de Naklili lo recibió con los brazos abiertos. Luego los familiares llegaron y lo observaron con asombro.

Naklili has come back from the dead!" they whispered. They sat at his feet as if he were a great man and waited for him to tell his story.

But Naklili, remembering Kati's warning, said nothing.

"Why won't you tell us your story, Naklili?" Naklili shook his head, unable to speak. The relatives began to be afraid.

In the weeks that followed, they spied on him when he went walking alone in the bush. "It must be that Naklili has come back from the dead to harm us," they told each other. Soon no one but his mother would speak with him.

Naklili became very lonely. He thought only of Kati. Even in the beautiful land of the living he could never be happy without her.

Naklili ha regresado de entre los muertos —cuchicheaban. Se sentaron a sus pies como si fuera un gran hombre y esperaron que les contara su historia.

Pero Naklili, recordando lo que Kati le había dicho, no les contó nada.

—¿Por qué no nos cuentas tu historia, Naklili? —Naklili sacudió la cabeza, sin poder decir nada. Los familiares comenzaron a asustarse.

Durante las semanas siguientes, lo espiaban mientras caminaba solo por los montes. —Seguramente Naklili ha regresado de entre los muertos para hacernos daño —se dijeron. Muy pronto, la única que le dirigía la palabra era su madre.

Naklili se sintió muy solo. Pensaba solamenta en Kati. Aun en la hermosa tierra de los vivos nunca podría estar contento sin ella.

One day Naklili got into his hammock and began to play his flute. He played and played until his mother and all his relatives came in from the plantation and gathered around.

They listened in amazement as Naklili told them everything that had happened. Finally, he explained that Kati had forbidden him to tell his story until he was ready to leave the land of the living forever.

Naklili's relatives were ashamed of having treated him so badly. "Don't leave us!" they pleaded.

But Naklili scarcely heard them. He was thinking only of Kati. He reached above the door for the string of beads she had left for him.

His relatives gasped in horror. Coiled just above Naklili's fingers was a poisonous snake. "Naklili!" they cried.

Un día, Naklili se echó en su hamaca y comenzó a tocar la flauta. Tocó y tocó hasta que su madre y todos sus familiares vinieron de la finca y se sentaron alrededor.

Todos escucharon maravillados mientras Naklili les contó todo lo que le había pasado. Por fin, les explicó que Kati le había prohibido que les contara su historia hasta que estuviera listo para dejar la tierra de los vivos para siempre.

Sus familiares estaban avergonzados de haberlo tratado tan mal. —¡No nos abandones! — rogaron.

Pero Naklili casi ni los escuchó. Estaba pensando solamente en Kati. Y alzó la mano para coger el collar de cuentas que ella le había dejado sobre el dintel de la puerta.

Sus familiares ahogaron gritos de espanto. Enroscada sobre la mano de Naklili había una serpiente venenosa. —¡Naklili! —gritaron.

29

But Naklili did not even feel the snake bite him. He heard Mother Scorpion call his name. He heard the spirits singing and dancing. He knew that Kati was waiting for him.

Pero Naklili ni siquiera sintió la picadura de la serpiente. Escuchó a la Madre Escorpión decir su nombre y escuchó a los espíritus que cantaban y bailaban. Sabía que Kati lo esperaba.

ABOUT THE STORY

IN THE EARLY 1900s, a young Jamaican missionary by the name of Dorminster Newton Wilson arrived on the Atlantic coast of Nicaragua. Over the years he wrote down the stories and customs of the Miskito Indians. A version of *Mother Scorpion Country* was one of the tales that he recorded.

The manuscript passed to his son after his death; it was never published. The story also disappeared from the oral tradition. By the 1930s, there was only a fragmentary mention of it in the anthropological literature. During the next fifty years of the Somoza dictatorship, popular culture was downgraded and neglected. By the time of my first visit to the Atlantic Coast of Nicaragua in 1983, none of the Miskito elders or scholars I spoke to had ever heard of Mother Scorpion Country.

Fortunately, in spite of wartime conditions in Nicaragua, the Ministry of Culture of the new Sandinista government had embarked upon an ambitious program of "rescuing the culture" of the peasants and indigenous peoples. Anthropologists were sent to interview elderly Miskitos and other minorities. Indians and Blacks were encouraged to be proud of their heritage.

In the context of this atmosphere of change, Bishop John Wilson of the Protestant Moravian Church, himself part Miskito, encouraged me in my project of recording and publishing the stories of the Atlantic Coast. Storytellers began to appear at Bishop John's house in Bluefields, Nicaragua. We sat outside until late into the night with Bishop John translating tales from Miskito to English which I recorded on my Sony recorder.

As I was about to head back to the United States, the Bishop recalled that his uncle, Mr. Cyril Wilson who lived in New York City, had an old manuscript that had been handed down to him by his father (the Bishop's grandfather), Dorminster Newton Wilson. Perhaps it would be of interest to me?

Mother Scorpion Country as you read it here is based on that original manuscript. Months of work went into researching concepts, clarifying details, reworking the language and the plot, all with the intent of staying as close as possible to the original story while making it lively and appropriate for today's young people.

Kati and Naklili are tragic lovers, reminiscent of Orpheus and Eurydice; yet the mood of the story is warm and loving. The dual perspective of the young couple provides a fascinating insight into the nature of life and death. The compassionate figure of Mother Scorpion reflects a pre-Christian matriarchal past.

San Francisco artist Virginia Stearns is well known for the archetypal images of her prints and "dreambooks." This is her first picture book for young people.

My thanks go to Bishop John Wilson, Cyril Wilson, Ray Hooker, David Schecter, Roxanne Dunbar Ortiz, Carlos Maibeth, Norma Smith, Larry Yep, Joanne Ryder and the many people of the Atlantic Coast of Nicaragua who offered their help and inspiration.

Harriet Rohmer
San Francisco, California
December, 1986